D1575550

From
Friend
To
Friend

A Special Gift

For

Yvonne Travis

From

Viola Perry

Date

12/5/02

Little Treasures Miniature Books

From Friend to Friend

Golden Moments—
Hope & Inspiration from Leaves of Gold

Precious Promises

Treasures from the Psalms

From
Friend
To
Friend

Edited by
Paul C. Brownlow

Brownlow

Brownlow Publishing Company, Inc.

*F*riend! How sacred the word. Born in the heart of God, and given to man as a treasure from the eternities— no word in the languages so heavily freighted with meaning.

With one friend I would count myself rich; to possess more than one, I were rich beyond comparison. A friend is a priceless gem for the crown of life here and a cherished star in memory forever.

— CYRUS B. NUBBAUM

*F*riends are in life's exchange
the sterling coin,
True tender for the rarest
forms of joy:
The only pauper is
the friendless man.

—Anonymous

A Friend in Need

"*A* friend in need,"
    my neighbor said to me—
"A friend indeed
    is what I mean to be;
In time of trouble
    I will come to you
And in the hour of need
    you'll find me true."

I thought a bit,
    and took him by the hand;
"My friend," said I,
    "you do not understand
The inner meaning
    of that simple rhyme—
A friend is what the heart
    needs all the time."

— HENRY VAN DYKE

*F*riendship is a sheltering tree;
Oh the joys that come down
shower-like.

— SAMUEL TAYLOR COLERIDGE

*E*ach friend represents a world in us,
a world possibly not born until they
arrive, and it is only by this meeting
that a new world is born.

— ANAÏS NIN

*T*he ornament of a house
is the friends that frequent it.

— Ralph Waldo Emerson

*W*ounds from a friend
can be trusted,
but an enemy multiplies kisses.

— Proverbs 27:6

No Fickle Shadow

The Shadow once said to its fellow-traveler: "No one is a friend like me. I follow you every step of the way. When you stand I am close by. When you walk I walk with you. When you run I keep stride with you. I am your constant companion. In sunlight or in moonlight I never forsake you."

The Body answered: "Yes, you go with me in sunlight and in moon light.

13

But where are you when neither the sun nor the moon shines upon me?"

A true friend, however, is no fickle shadow. His constancy is not dependent on fair weather. His love is higher than the clouds. His relationship with you is governed by that which is within him— not exterior circumstances. Consequently, he will stick with you when the earth shakes and trembles and the storm clouds blot out the sun, the moon and the stars.

In olden times John Huss had such a friend. When he was on his way to the stake to be burned, an old friend stepped out from among the sightseers and gripped his hand without saying a word. Huss turned and said that only God and himself knew how much that handclasp meant in the painful hour.

Such a friend is our stay in life and in death.

*T*rue friends have no solitary joys or sorrows. Both are shared. In the hour of peace and gladness, what is our want? Friendship. When our hearts overflow with gratitude, what is our need? A friend. When distress haunts us and misery walks by our side, where do we turn? To friends. When our

hearts bleed and our sacred emotion
finds no utterance, what does our
heart long for? Friends. Friends to
share. Friends to bear.

*G*reater love
has no one than this,
that he lay down his life
for his friends.

— JOHN 15:13

17

*T*o be unselfish in everything,
especially in love and friendship,
was my highest pleasure,
my maxim, my discipline.

— GOETHE

*T*he shifts of fortune test
the reliability of friends.

— CICERO

In Tune

I don't remember when I first began to call you "friend."

One day, I only know, the vague companionship that I'd seen grow so imperceptibly, turned gold, and ran in tune with all I'd thought or dared to plan.

Since then, you've been to me like music, low, yet clear; a fire that throws its warm, bright glow on me as on each

woman, child, and man, and common thing that lies within its rays;

You've been like wholesome food that stays the cry of hungry, groping minds; and like a star—A self-sufficient star— you make me raise my utmost being to a higher sky, in tune, like you, with earth, yet wide, and far.

— FLORENCE STEIGERWALT

My friend, judge not me,
Thou seest I judge not thee.

— WILLIAM CAMDEN

He is a friend who,
in dubious circumstances,
aids in deeds when deeds
are necessary.

— PLAUTUS

*F*riends are too valuable not to hold them close to the soul. That being where they belong, we should do more than keep a precious place reserved for them— we should grip them with our love, thoughtfulness and gratitude. They can be held. For the right kind of people are not apt to pull away from a person who demonstrates that he is on their side.

—Anonymous

*F*riendship, like the immortality of the soul, is too good to be believed. When friendships are real, they are not glass threads or frostwork, but the solidest thing we know.

— RALPH WALDO EMERSON

*T*hey are rich who have friends.
— SCANDINAVIAN PROVERB

*F*riendship that follows from the heart cannot be frozen by adversity, as the water that flows from the spring cannot congeal in winter.

— JAMES FENIMORE COOPER

*F*ate chooses our relatives, we choose our friends.

— JACQUES DELILLE

A Rose to the Living

A rose to the living is more than
Sumptuous wreaths to the dead;
In filling love's infinite store,
A rose to the living is more,
If graciously given before
The hungering spirit is fed—
A rose to the living is more than
Sumptuous wreaths to the dead.

— NIXON WATERMAN

*Y*es'm old friends is always best,
'less you can catch a new one
that's fit to make an old one out of.

— SARAH ORNE JEWETT

A man that has friends must
show himself friendly: and there is a
friend that sticks closer than a brother.

— PROVERBS 18:24

A Precious Part Of Me

"*I* am a part of all whom I have met,"
So, friend of mine,
   you are a wholesome part;
Our precious visits,
   lingering with me yet,
Are flowers in the
   garden of my heart.

Your smiles like violets,
  sweet beyond compare,
Your words, carnations,
  cheering on my way,
Your deeds like roses,
  rich with perfume rare,
Bring faith and hope
  and love every day.

So, friend of mine,
  though you are far away,
Between us may stretch
  mountain, plain, or sea,
Yet by my side you walk
  and talk each day,
Because you are a precious
  part of me.

— CHARLES ELMER CHAPLER

29

*F*or none of us lives
to himself alone
and none of us dies
to himself alone.

— ROMANS 14:7

*T*wo are better than one.

— ECCLESIASTES 4:9

30

For the Love of a Friend

O, for the love of a friend whose voice and touch will rainbow sorrows, diamond tears, making of them gems of rarest joy; one who forgives all my shortages ere asked to do so; one who dares to the uttermost of human imagery; one whose ship will cast anchor, and throw out the life line of hope when storms are near; one who

forgives in me all that I can forgive in myself. O, for the love of a friend who can be made the sacred trustee of my heart; one who is more to me than the closest relative; one whose very name is so sacred that I want to whisper it softly; one who lingers near my door in time of distress, and stretches forth his hand, which is not empty or cold, and who says little, but feels largely.

— MAE LAWSON

*T*he loftiest friendships have no commercial element in them; to the contrary, they are founded on sacrifice. They neither expect nor desire gift for gift or service for service. No bushel of friendship for a bushel of favors.

— SARAH B. COOPER

*G*o often to the house of thy friend, for weeds choke up the unused path.

— SCANDINAVIAN PROVERB

The Things I Prize

These are the things I prize
        And hold of dearest worth:
Light of the sapphire skies,
        Peace of the silent hills,
Shelter of the forests,
        Comfort of the grass,
Music of birds,
        Murmurs of little rills,
Shadows of clouds
        That swiftly pass,

And, after showers,
   The smell of flowers
And of the good brown earth,—
   And best of all, along the way,
Friendship and mirth.

— HENRY VAN DYKE

*F*riendship is a word,
the very sight of which in print
makes the heart warm.

— AUGUSTINE BIRRELL

True Beat of Our Heart

What is the best a friend can be
To any soul, to you or me?
Not only shelter, comfort, rest—
    Inmost refreshment unexpressed;
Not only a beloved guide
    To thread life's labyrinth
        at our side,
Or with love's torch lead on before;
    Though these be much,
        there yet is more.

The best friend is an atmosphere
    Warm with all inspirations dear,
Wherein we breath the large,
        free breath
Of life that hath no taint of death.
Our friend is an unconscious PART
        OF EVERY TRUE BEAT
            OF OUR HEART;
    A strength, a growth,
            whence we derive
Feelings that keep the world alive.

*F*riendship renders
prosperity more brilliant,
while it lightens adversity
by sharing it and making
its burdens common.

— CICERO

*T*rue friendship is no gourd,
springing in a night
and withering in a day.

— CHARLOTTE BRONTE

We Call It Friendship

*T*he need for friends is imperative. It is not good for us to be friendless. We were made to give and to receive, to help and to be helped, to encourage and to be encouraged— to feel a bond with others. Standing alone can never satisfy. Our nature requires a tie to faithful others. We call it friendship.

— LEROY BROWNLOW

*Y*ou must therefore, love me,
myself, and not my circumstances,
if we are to be real friends.

— CICERO

*L*ife hath no blessing
like a prudent friend.

— EURIPIDES

*S*omething like home that is not home is to be desired, it is found in the house of a friend.

— Sir W. Temple

*L*earn to greet your friends with a smile; they carry too many frowns in their own heart to be bothered with yours.

— Mary Allette Ayer

More Precious Than Gold

*F*riendship is more precious than gold. There is no one so poor that he is not rich if he has a friend; there is no one so rich that he is not poor without a friend.

It is not fancy imagination or vain words, but rather the golden strand linking lives forged from untarnished mettle. It is like the rope mountain

climbers use to bind themselves for safety and progress.

Real friendship is abiding. Like charity, it suffers long and is kind. Like love, vaunteth not itself, but pursues the even tenor of its way, unaffrighted by ill-report, loyal in adversity, the shining jewel of happy days.

Friendship is a gift, but it is also an acquirement.

It is a sort of Divinity which hovers over two hearts.

*F*riendship hath the skill and observance of the best physician; the diligence and vigilance of the best nurse; and the tenderness and patience of the best mother.

—LORD CLARENDON

*T*o him that is afflicted, pity should be showed from his friend.

— JOB 6:14

*G*o home to your family and tell them how much the Lord has done for you, and how he has had mercy on you.

— MARK 5:19

*T*o have a friend is to have one of the sweetest gifts that life can bring; to be a friend is to have a solemn and tender education of soul from day to day.

— AMY ROBERTSON BROWN

45

A Friend Is A Person...

Who will help you in
the hour of sickness;
Who will help you up the hill
when you are sliding down;
Who will defend you in the hour
when others speak evil of you;
Who will believe in your innocence
until you admit your guilt.
Who will say behind your back
what he says to your face;

Who will shake hands with you
wherever he meets you, even
though you wear patches; and
Who will do all these things
without expecting any return.

— DOROTHY C. RETSLOFF

*A*nimals are such agreeable
friends, they ask no questions,
they pass no criticisms.

— GEORGE ELIOT

We cannot tell the precise moment when friendship is formed. As in filling a vessel drop by drop, there is at last a drop which makes it run over; so in a series of kindnesses there is at last one which makes the heart run over.

— SAMUEL JOHNSON

No life is so strong and complete, But it yearns for the smile of a friend.

— WALLACE BRUCE

The Love of a Friend

*F*riendship—
Like music heard on the waters,
Like pines when the wind passeth by,
Like pearls in the depths of the ocean,
Like stars that enamel the sky,
Like June and the odor of roses,
Like dew and the freshness of morn,
Like sunshine that kisseth the clover,
Like tassels of silk on the corn,

Like mountains that arch the
blue heavens,
Like clouds when the sun dippeth low,
Like songs of birds in the forest,
Like brooks where the
sweet waters flow,
Like dreams of Arcadian pleasures,
Like colors that gratefully blend,
Like everything breathing of kindness,
Like these is the love of a friend.

— A.P. STANLEY

*D*o not use a hatchet to remove a fly from your friend's forehead.

— CHINESE PROVERB

*Y*ou can always tell a real friend: when you've made a fool of yourself, he doesn't feel you've done a permanent job.

— LAURENCE J. PETER

*O*ne friend in a lifetime is much; two are many; three are hardly possible.

— HENRY ADAMS

*S*o long as we love we serve; so long as we are loved by others, I would almost say that we are indispensable; and no man is useless while he has a friend.

— ROBERT LOUIS STEVENSON

*I*f a man does not make new acquaintances as he advances through life, he will soon find himself left alone. A man, sir, should keep his friendship in a constant repair.

— SAMUEL JOHNSON

A friend is the gift of God, and He only who made hearts can unite them.

— SOUTHEY

Wealth may crumble like some shaken tower, but friendship still remains. Disaster and defeat may overtake us and, like a shadow, hide our star, and our ambitions turn to ashes on our lips; but friendship, like some guardian angel, rekindles and fans into life the hope which had almost fled.

I would not live
without the love of my friends.

— JOHN KEATS

*T*he comfort of having a friend may
be taken away, but not that of having
had one.

— SENECA

So shall a friendship fill each heart
With perfume sweet as roses are,
That even though we be apart,
We'll scent the fragrance from afar.

— GEORGIA McCOY

Friendship is love
without wings.

— BYRON

The Friendly Things

*O*h, it's just the little homely things,
The unobtrusive, friendly things,
The "Won't-you-let-me-help-you" things
That make our pathway light.

The "Laugh-with-me-it's-funny" things
And it's the jolly, joking things,
The "Never-mind-the-trouble" things
That makes the world seem bright.

For all the countless famous things
The wondrous record-breaking things,
These "never-can-be-equaled" things
That all the papers cite.

Are not the little human things,
The "everyday encountered" things,
The "just-because-I-like-you" things,
That make us happy quite.

So here's to all the little things,
The "done-and-then-forgotten" things,
Those "oh-it's-simply-nothing" things
That make life worth the fight.

— AUTHOR UNKNOWN

*T*here is no folly equal to that of
throwing away friendship, in a world
where friendship is so rare.

— BULWER-LYTON

*F*riendship is the marriage
of the soul.

*T*he most I can do for my friend is
simply to be his friend. I have no
wealth to bestow upon him. If he
knows that I am happy in loving him
he will want no other reward. Is not
friendship divine in this?

— LAVATIN

Make Me Worthy

*I*t is my joy in life to find
At every turning of the road
The strong arms of a comrade kind
To help me onward with my load;
And since I have no gold to give,
And love alone must make amends,
My only prayer is, while I live—
God make me worthy
Of my friends.

— Frank Dempster Sherman

*T*wo friends, two bodies
with one soul inspired.

— ALEXANDER POPE

*B*e slow in choosing a friend,
slower in changing.

— BENJAMIN FRANKLIN

The Blessings of Friendship

*T*here are friends who are to us like a great rock in a weary land. We flee to them in the heat of parching days and rest in their shadow. A friend in whom we can confide without fear of disappointment; who, we are sure, will never fail us, will never stint his love in serving us, who always has healing tenderness of the hurt of our heart,

comfort for our sorrow, and cheer for
our discouragement, such a friend is
not only a rock of shelter to us in time
of danger, but is also as rivers of water
in a thirsty land, when our hearts cry
out for life and love.

— J.R. MILLER

A friend loveth at all times,
and a brother is born for adversity.

— PROVERBS 17:17

There are no rules of friendship; it must be left to itself; we cannot force it any more than love.

— HAZLITT

Rejoice with those who rejoice; mourn with those who mourn.

— ROMANS 12:15

*T*hus, God's bright sunshine over-
head, God's flowers beside your feet,
The path of life that you must tread
Can little hold of fear or dread:
And by such pleasant pathways led,
May all your life be sweet.

— HELEN WAITHMAN

We can never replace a friend. When a man is fortunate enough to have several, he finds they are all different; no one has a double in friendship.

— SCHILLER

Do not judge,
or you too will be judged.

— MATTHEW 7:1

*A*ll who would win joy, must share it; happiness was born a twin.

— LORD BYRON

*O*ther blessings may be taken away, but if we have acquired a good friend by goodness, we have a blessing which improves in value when others fail. It is even heightened by sufferings.

— W.E. CHANNING

The Language of Friendship

*F*riendship takes place between those who have an affinity for one another, and is a perfectly natural and inevitable result. No professions or advances will avail. Even speech, at first, necessarily has nothing to do with it; but it follows after silence, as the buds in the graft do not put forth

into leaves till long after the graft has taken. It is a drama in which the parties have no part to act. . . .

Friendship is never established as an understood relation. Do you demand that I be less your friend that you may know it? Yet what right have I to think that another cherishes so rare a sentiment for me? It is a miracle which requires constant proofs. It is an exercise of the finest imagination and the rarest faith. It says by a silent but

eloquent behavior: "I will be so related to thee as thou canst not imagine; even so thou mayest believe, I will spend truth, all my wealth on thee," and the friend responds silently through his nature, and life, and treats his friend with the same divine courtesy. . . .

The language of friendship is not words but meaning. It s an intelligence above language.

— HENRY DAVID THOREAU

*O*f all happiness, the most charming is that of a firm and gentle friendship. It sweetens all our cares, dispels our sorrows, and counsels us in all extremities. Nay, if there were no other comfort in it than the bare exercise of so generous a virtue, even for that single reason a man would not be without it.

— SENECA

A friend is, as it were,
a second self.

— CICERO

*T*raveling in the company of those
we love is home in motion.

— LEIGH HUNT

I no doubt deserved my enemies, but
I don't believe I deserved my friends.

— WALT WHITMAN

When Friends
Walk By Our Side

When good friends walk beside us,
On the trails that we must keep,
Our burdens seem less heavy,
And the hills are not so steep,
The weary miles pass swiftly,
Taken in a joyous stride,
And all the world seems brighter,
When friends walk by our side.

— AUTHOR UNKNOWN

Sweet Is the Journey

*F*riendship is a chain of gold
Shaped in God's all perfect mold
Each link a smile, a laugh, a tear
A grip of the hand, a word of cheer
Steadfast as the ages roll
Binding closer soul to soul
No matter how far or heavy the load
Sweet is the journey on friendship's
   road.

— AUTHOR UNKNOWN

Decorated With Friends

Your house will look better, if you decorate it with friends. They are the ornaments that will give it more attraction and cheer than all others combined. Nothing is comparable to the living ornaments that breathe so much warmth into plain quarters.

Grandmother's little farm house was a classic example. I have a picture of

that old place, but I have a clearer picture in my album of precious memories. That little humble abode was inexpensive and unpretentious. No plumbing. No electricity. Only one carpet she made by hand. But it had a big cook stove and a big dining table. It was a common practice for her house to be adorned with the unexcelled beauty of pleasant friends. When I was a child we went there almost every Sunday. There was love. There was joy.

It was there that we experienced the spirit-lifting feeling that lumber and nails, brick and mortar, can never give. It had what mansions often lack— love! friendship! That country home had a touch of warm, pulsating beauty that only people can give four walls. The warmth and joy I found there made it a place of priceless attraction.

*H*old a true friend
with both your hands.

— NIGERIAN PROVERB

*P*erfume and incense bring joy to
the heart, and the pleasantness of
one's friend springs from his earnest
counsel.

— PROVERBS 27:9

*T*he years. . .
    Have taught some sweet,
Some bitter lessons,
    None wiser than this,—
To spend all things else,
    But of old friends
To be most miserly.

— JAMES RUSSELL LOWELL

*P*eace to you. The friends here send their greeting. Greet the friends there by name.

— 3 John 14

*F*riendship improves happiness, and abates misery, by doubling our joy, and dividing our grief.

— Joseph Addison

81

Stronger Than Kinship

*F*riendship has been called the love without flowers or veils. It shelters like the outstretched branches of a full-leafed tree. Friendship preserves companionship. It is stronger than kindred. It is more generous than kindness. It has no savor of concession or patronage.

Wise men use the eyes of friends as lenses through which to better scan

their horizon and more accurately chart the seas they sail. For "there is a power in love to divine another's destiny better than the other can, and by heroic encouragement hold him to his tasks."

Friendship is sincere. It scorns flattery. It faces facts. It is a lift. It soon stops when it is begun for an end. It is not a thing to be hurried. Rush it and it soon gets out of breath.

Like health, the wealth of friendship

is seldom fully appraised until lost. Then its value floats before us like the vision in a mirage. The light of friendship is like the phosphorous in the sea, seen plainest when all about is dark.

Friendship is like a staunch ship, character built, so well balanced it rests evenly on its keel and rides all storms, a ship that is propelled by the heart, and piloted by the intellect.

Pure friendship is something which men of limited intellect seldom experi-

ence. As Samuel Johnson said:

> Friendship, peculiar boon of Heaven,
> The noble mind's delight and pride,
> To men and angels only given,
> To all the lower world denied.

— ADAPTED, R.L. JONES

Give me a few friends who will love me for what I am, or am not, and keep ever burning before my wondering steps the kindly light of hope. And though age and infirmity overtake me, and I come not in sight of the castle of my dreams; teach me still to be thankful for life and time's old memories that are good and sweet. And may the evening twilight find me gentle still.

— AUTHOR UNKNOWN

*F*riendship is always
a sweet responsibility,
never an opportunity.

— KAHIL GIBRAN

*F*riendship is love
with understanding.

— ANCIENT PROVERB

*T*he best rule of friendship is to keep your heart a little softer than your head.

— GEORGE SANTAYANA

*H*appy is the house that shelters a friend.

— RALPH WALDO EMERSON

By Being Yourself

I love you, not only for what you
re, but for what I am when I am with
ou.

I love you, not only for what you have
ade of yourself, but for what you are
aking of me.

I love you for the part of me that you
ring out; I love you for putting your
and into my heaped-up heart and

passing over all the foolish, weak
things that you can't help dimly seeing
there, and for drawing out into the
light all the beautiful belongings that
no one else has looked quite far
enough to find.

I love you because you are helping to
make of the lumber of my life not a tav-
ern but a temple; out of the works of
my every day not a reproach but a
song.

I love you because you have done

more than any creed could have done
to make me good, and more than any
fate could have done to make me
happy.

You have done it by being yourself.
Perhaps that is what being a friend
means, after all.

— ROY CROFT

The friendship of the good, and of those who have the same virtues, is perfect friendship. Such friendships, therefore, endure so long as each retains his character and virtue is a lasting thing.

— ARISTOTLE

Friendship consists in forgetting what one gives and remembering what one receives.

— ALEXANDER DUMAS THE YOUNGER

*F*riendship cannot rise on the ladder of perfection. Shortcomings and weaknesses are the common lot of us all. And this is one of the reasons we need each other. If we were perfect, the need would not be so urgent.

—LEROY BROWNLOW

*T*rue friendship comes when silence between two people is comfortable.

— DAVE TYSON GENTRY

I desire so to conduct the affairs of this administration that if at the end, when I come to lay down the reins of power, I have lost every other friend on earth, I shall at least have one friend left, and that friend shall be down inside me.

—ABRAHAM LINCOLN

Today

*O*ur friendship cannot rely on our past together. And it cannot rely on the future we anticipate. It must be now. It must be today. For our past is only precious memories, and our future is still misty imaginings. Can't we find time to be together today?

—MARY HOLLINGSWORTH

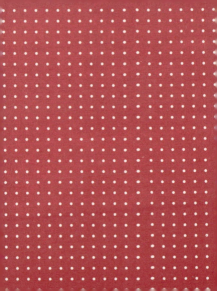